EVERYDAY ECONOMICS
BANKING

Heather C. Hudak

Weigl Publishers Inc.

Published by Weigl Publishers Inc.
350 5th Avenue, Suite 3304, PMB 6G
New York, NY 10118-0069

Website: www.weigl.com
Copyright ©2010 Weigl Publishers Inc.
All rights reserved. No part of this publication may be reproduced, stored in a retrieval system, or transmitted in any form or by any means, electronic, mechanical, photocopying, recording, or otherwise, without the prior written permission of the publisher.

Hudak, Heather C., 1975-
 Banking / Heather C. Hudak.
      p. cm. -- (Everyday economics)
 Includes index.
 ISBN 978-1-60596-651-9 (hard cover : alk. paper) -- ISBN 978-1-60596-652-6 (soft cover : alk. paper)
 1. Banks and banking--Juvenile literature. I. Title.
 HG1609.H83 2010
 332.1--dc22
                           2009008365

Printed in China
1 2 3 4 5 6 7 8 9 0   13 12 11 10 09

Every reasonable effort has been made to trace ownership and to obtain permission to reprint copyright material. The publishers would be pleased to have any errors or omissions brought to their attention so that they may be corrected in subsequent printings.

Weigl acknowledges Getty Images as its primary image supplier for this title.

Project Coordinator **Heather C. Hudak** | Designer **Terry Paulhus** | Layout **Terry Paulhus**

All of the Internet URLs given in the book were valid at the time of publication. However, due to the dynamic nature of the Internet, some addresses may have changed, or sites may have ceased to exist since publication. While the author and publisher regret any inconvenience this may cause readers, no responsibility for any such changes can be accepted by either the author or the publisher.

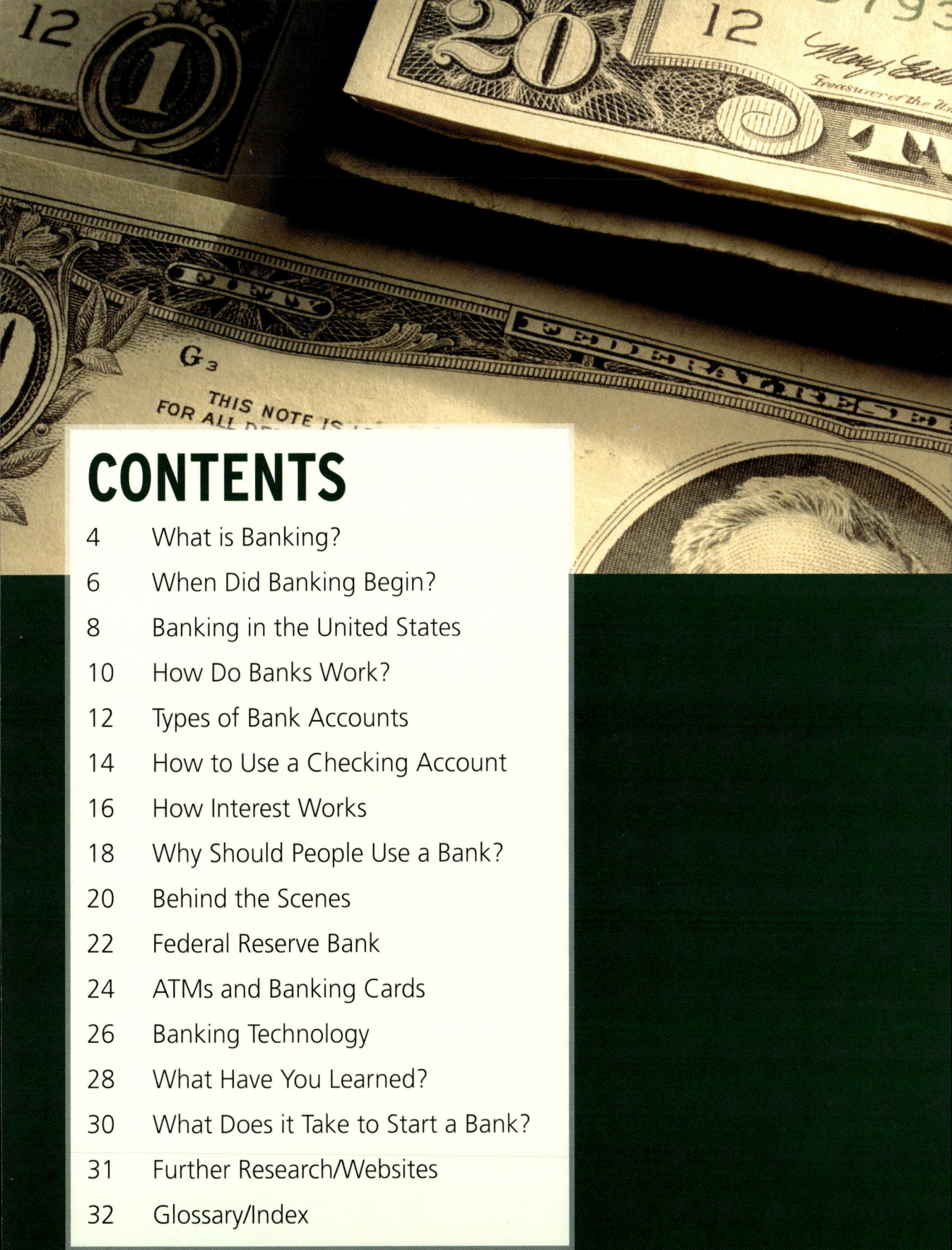

CONTENTS

4	What is Banking?
6	When Did Banking Begin?
8	Banking in the United States
10	How Do Banks Work?
12	Types of Bank Accounts
14	How to Use a Checking Account
16	How Interest Works
18	Why Should People Use a Bank?
20	Behind the Scenes
22	Federal Reserve Bank
24	ATMs and Banking Cards
26	Banking Technology
28	What Have You Learned?
30	What Does it Take to Start a Bank?
31	Further Research/Websites
32	Glossary/Index

BANKING VOCABULARY

BONDS money a person lends to a company that earns more money over time

DEPOSIT the act of putting money into a bank account; the sum of money in the account

INSURED made arrangements to be repaid if money is damaged or stolen

INTEREST money paid at a regular rate for the use of a loan

INVESTING purchasing an item with the hope that it will be worth more someday

LEND to give something, such as money, with the understanding that it will be returned

STOCKS a piece, or share, of a company you can buy, represented by a certificate

TRANSFERRED moved funds from one person or business to another

What is Banking?

Banking is a system people, businesses, and governments use to manage money. Banks are financial institutions in which people can **deposit** their money for later use. People also can borrow money from banks. They may use this money to make major purchases, such as cars or houses.

Banks offer many services. These include accounts where people can deposit and save money, accounts that can be used for purchases, and loaning money.

When people put money in a bank, they know their funds are safe. Banks are **insured** against theft and other events, such as fire. They make sure that money is sent, or **transferred**, to other people or businesses in a way that is legal.

4

■ Banking can be done on street corners using computerized Automated Teller Machines (ATMs).

Banks **lend** people money to invest in large purchases. Loans and mortgages are two of the most common ways to borrow from a bank. Banks lend this money to people for a certain period of time. During this time, the money is paid back in one or more payments each month. Banks charge a fee for borrowing money. This fee is a form of **interest**. It is a percentage of the amount borrowed.

Investing is a service banks offer. This is when a certain amount of money is used to buy **stocks** or **bonds**. The hope is that the stocks and bonds will increase in value over a period of time.

■ Cities have many different banks to help people manage money.

5

BANKING VOCABULARY

BARTER to trade goods and services for other goods and services

CENTRAL BANK a bank that provides services for the nation's government

COMMERCIAL for the purpose of making a profit

COMMODITIES items of value

CURRENCY the type of money used in a certain country

EXCHANGE to give something and receive another

REGULATE control or maintain

When Did Banking Begin?

Throughout history, banks have played an important role in the way people **exchange** goods and services.

10,000-6000 BC People begin trading cows, grain, and other **commodities** for goods and services in a **barter** system.

650 BC People begin making coins to exchange for goods and services.

800 AD Paper money is first used by the Chinese to avoid carrying heavy coins over long distances.

1609 The Bank of Amsterdam is established. It is thought to be the first public bank and is used by Dutch merchants. It sets the groundwork for **commercial** banking.

10,000-6000 BC   650 BC   1609 AD

1791 The First Bank of the United States, a **central bank**, is created. The country now has a firm banking system, a supply of money, and its own **currency**.

1811 The First Bank of the United States is dismantled.

1816 President Madison signs a bill to form the Second Bank of the United States. It is shut down in 1836.

1840 There are about 700 banks in the United States.

1907 Successful private banker J.P. Morgan organizes a group of bankers to act as a central bank to help put an end to the financial crisis of the time.

1913 The Federal Reserve Act is passed, and 12 federal banks are spread across the country to supervise private banks and monitor payment systems.

1920 There are more than 30,000 commercial banks doing business in the United States.

1934 A U.S. central bank is formed to **regulate** banking systems across the nation.

1816   1907   1920

Banking in the United States

BANKING VOCABULARY

BANKNOTES paper money that acts as a promise to pay the sum upon request

RESERVES money on hold

In the early days of banking in the United States, banks gave people papers called **banknotes** in exchange for their money. At any time, a person could trade their banknotes for silver or gold.

After the second central bank closed in 1836, state governments began monitoring banks. It was the government's job to make sure banks had enough silver and gold to trade for the banknotes they issued. Sometimes, this was not the case. People would try to trade their notes, and the bank could not give them the funds.

People have been keeping money in banks in the United States for hundreds of years.

In 1863, the National Bank Act was passed. It established a system of national banks that regulated the banking system across the nation. National banknotes were made so that all banks used the same system. This system worked well.

People who put their money in a bank trust the bank will take care of their money. Even though banks lend their clients' money to others, clients can withdraw their money at any time.

Banks have a certain amount of cash, or **reserves**, on hand at all times. They have about three to 10 percent of the money they receive through deposits. If everyone who used that bank decided to withdraw their money at the same time, it would not be possible. Banks often lend more money than they have on site.

The First Bank of the United States was located in Philadelphia, Pennsylvania.

9

BANKING VOCABULARY

CREDITED added to the sum of an account
DEBIT CARD a plastic card that is issued by a bank to a client that allows the client to access his or her account
DEDUCTED taken away or subtracted from an account
PROFIT money earned
WITHDRAWN taken out of any account

How do Banks Work?

In the United States, there are two basic ways banks work. The money a person deposits in the bank is pooled with the money other people deposit. The bank uses this money to make more money, or a **profit**. Banks do this by lending deposited money to others. Banks make money, or interest, on the money they lend. They pay a small portion of this interest to account holders for using their money. The bank keeps the rest.

Next, banks use a system of exchanging money for goods and services. The money deposited is **credited** to the account. Money that is **withdrawn** or spent using checks or a **debit card** is **deducted** from the account. Banks often charge a fee when clients use these services. This is another way they make money.

What happens when banks lend money to clients?

People deposit their money into a bank.

INDIVIDUALS

Banks make a profit by lending their clients' money to businesses or other clients.

BANK

BUSINESSES

Businesses and borrowers pay interest to banks.

Banks pay interest to people for the money they deposit.

10

Types of Banks

There are many types of banks. These are just a few examples.

Retail Banks
These are the most common kinds of banks. Retail banks can be found in shopping malls or in local communities. Most people have a personal savings and checking account at a retail bank.

Central Banks
Central banks are organizations that manage banking activities. In the United States, the Federal Reserve is the central bank.

Commercial Banks
Commercial banks provide services to businesses. Businesses have different needs, such as more deposits, than individuals. For this reason, special services are offered at these banks. However, commercial banks often are part of a retail bank.

Credit Unions
Credit unions are very similar to retail banks. The main difference is that credit unions are owned by their customers. Credit unions have limits on who can use their services. Customers usually have something in common, such as the place where they work or the community where they live. Only people belonging to these groups can put their money in a credit union. Credit unions are nonprofit. This means they are not looking to make extra money. As a result, they often have lower fees and pay higher interest for money deposited.

BANKING VOCABULARY

BALANCE the amount of money in an account

CLEARED free of any reason why the money cannot be moved from one account to another

INCENTIVE encouragement for someone to do something

STATEMENT a document that shows all of the transactions, such as deposits and withdrawals, that have taken place over a period of time

TRANSACTIONS acts of business, such as buying or selling

Types of Bank Accounts

There are many types of banks accounts. Each has different rules and interest rates. Some of the most common types of accounts are savings, checking, and certificates of deposit.

Savings Accounts

If people want to save money rather than spend it, it can be deposited in a savings account. Funds in a savings account earn interest as **incentive** for people to keep their money in the bank. Sometimes, money must remain in the bank for a certain length of time before it can be withdrawn. In other cases, banks may require a minimum **balance** to be in the account, or they may charge the account holder for withdrawing money. These guides are in place to help people increase their savings. A bank **statement** is provided for all savings accounts.

George Washington is featured on the one dollar bill.

Checking Accounts

To use money to make purchases and other **transactions**, a person can use a checking account. Money in a checking account earns very little interest or none at all. However, the account holder can write checks to pay for goods and services rather than use cash. Checks can only be written for the amount of money that is in the account. If the amount on the check is higher than the balance, it will not be **cleared**. A fee will be charged for writing a "bad" check. A debit card also can be used to withdraw cash or to pay for items from a checking account. Keeping a record of the money deposited and withdrawn will show how much money is in the account. Banks can also provide a statement of debits and credits for the account.

Certificates of Deposit (CD)

A CD is a high-interest account that can be Federal Deposit Insurance Corporation (FDIC) insured. CDs earn more interest than regular savings accounts. They often require a minimum balance and require that the money cannot be withdrawn during a certain period of time.

COMPARISON CHART		
Features	Savings	Checking
Minimum Deposit	✓	
Statements	✓	✓
Interest	✓	✓
Fee for Withdrawal	✓	
Checks		✓
Minimum Balance	✓	
Useful for Purchases		✓
Incentives to Save	✓	

13

BANKING VOCABULARY

ENDORSED signed the back of the check to authorize release of funds

How to Use a Checking Account

Checking accounts are ideal for people who want to keep their money safe until they plan to spend.

Once a person has opened a checking account, he or she will need to deposit cash and checks into the account. Often, cash can be withdrawn immediately from the account. To deposit a check, it needs to be **endorsed**. Once a check has been endorsed, anyone can cash it. After the check has been deposited, it may take a few days before the money can be used. This is because the check needs to be cleared.

Account holders may be charged a fee for a checking account. This helps the bank pay for its services. Each time a check or a debit card is used, the account holder may have to pay a small amount.

Writing a Check

Checks can be written so long as there is money in the checking account. If there is not enough money in the account to cover the amount written on the check, the check will "bounce." The check will be sent back unpaid, and the check writer will be charged a penalty fee for writing a check that bounces.

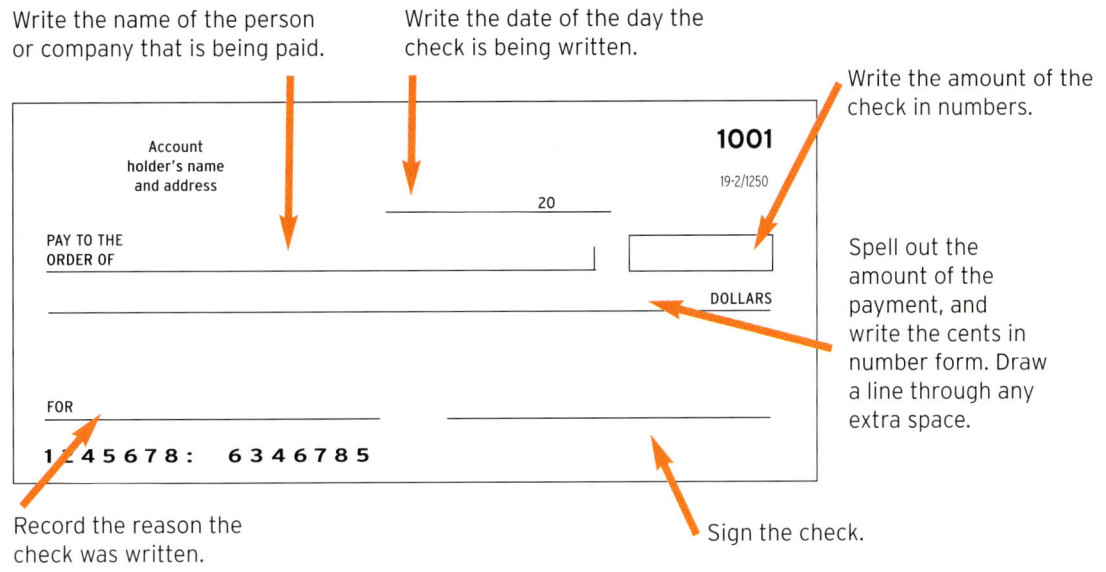

Write the name of the person or company that is being paid.

Write the date of the day the check is being written.

Write the amount of the check in numbers.

Spell out the amount of the payment, and write the cents in number form. Draw a line through any extra space.

Record the reason the check was written.

Sign the check.

Using Your Check Register

A book called a check register can be used to keep track of the ways money is deposited and spent from a checking account. Each time the account is used, the account holder writes in the check register.

The number code refers to the check number or the debit transaction number. Write a "D" for deposit or "T" for transfer.

In the date column, write the month, day, and year that the transaction was made.

Write a brief sentence describing the transaction in the Transaction Description section.

Payment Amount should be filled in if the account was used to purchase, withdraw, or transfer cash.

Deposit Amount is filled in when money is put into the account.

Add deposits and subtract withdrawals from the previous balance in the account, and write the new total in the Balance column.

Each month, a bank statement is sent to the account holder. Compare the transactions in the check register to those on the statement to be sure they match.

Number or Code	Date	Transaction Description	Payment Amount	Deposit Amount	$ Balance

15

BANKING VOCABULARY

PRINCIPLE the value of money borrowed before interest
DEBTS money owed

How Interest Works

Interest is a fee that is charged for borrowing money. Interest works in two ways.

First, banks charge interest on the money they lend. Banks take a risk when they lend money. The borrower may not be able to pay back what he or she takes. People must pay a fee for every dollar they borrow. The money they borrow is called the **principle**.

People who borrow money over a longer period of time pay higher rates than those who borrow money for a shorter period of time. This is because the bank is taking a risk for a longer time. Rates also are higher for people who have had trouble paying their **debts** in the past. How many people want to borrow money and how much money the bank has to lend both affect the interest rate.

Interest is a way to earn money on the balance of a savings account.

The more money a bank has, the lower its interest rate will be. If many people want to borrow money, the rates will increase. This follows the rules of supply and demand.

Supply refers to the amount of a product or service that is available for people to buy. Demand is how much of that product or service people actually want to buy. If there is too much supply and not enough demand, prices will be lower. More demand and lower supply increases prices.

In the same way that people pay banks for borrowing money, banks pay people for using their money. The bank then lends this money to other people.

FAQ

What is simple interest?
Simple interest is a flat rate paid on money borrowed. Assume the interest is 15 percent per year. If a person borrows $100, she would pay $15 in interest at the end of the year. Fifteen percent of the original amount borrowed is added each year if that the money remains unpaid. After two years, she would pay $30 in interest and $45 after three years.

What is compound interest?
Compound interest is paid on the money a person borrows, as well as interest and other fees. Again, assume the interest rate is 15 percent per year, and the person has borrowed $100. After one year, he simply pays $15 in interest. However, the following year, he will pay 15 percent interest on the current balance of $115. The balance owing after two years is $132.25 and $152.09 after three years.

BANKING VOCABULARY

BILLS money owed for the use of goods or services

Why Should People Use a Bank?

In most cases, money in a bank is safe. The Federal Deposit Insurance Corporation (FDIC) is a U.S. government department that encourages people to use banks by insuring the money stored there. The FDIC insures an account holder's banked money up to $250,000. Money in a wallet or piggy bank is not insured. If the money is lost, stolen, or damaged, it cannot be replaced.

Banks are the most common place to save money and make transactions. People can make money on the funds they keep in a bank. Banks pay a fee just to hold money. The money in the piggy bank or wallet never grows.

■ Banks help keep money safe from loss, theft, or damage.

It is much easier to transfer money through a bank. It is much safer to write a check or use a debit card than to carry large amounts of uninsured cash. As well, people can pay many of their **bills** through the bank. This is easier than mailing money to many different places.

The bank keeps records of all transactions as proof they took place. Money that is mailed or carried in a wallet can get lost or stolen, and there is no record of the transaction.

FAQ

How do people choose a bank?
Some people choose a bank that is easy to access, such as one that is online or in their neighborhood. It is also possible to check out a bank's website to see the services it offers. Comparing more than one bank can provide a wealth of information about the types of accounts they offer for children or students, as well as interest rates and other services. Visiting a branch to see if the staff is friendly and able to answer questions may be useful when selecting a bank.

How do people choose an account?
Before choosing an account type, people must decide what they want to do with their money. Do they need to pay bills? Will they be making purchases using checks? Would they like to save for the future? Remember, some accounts must have a minimum balance or the bank will charge fees for services. These things should all be considered before picking a bank account.

Behind the Scenes

Once money is deposited in a bank, it can be loaned to others. This diagram shows how this process works.

How does interest work?

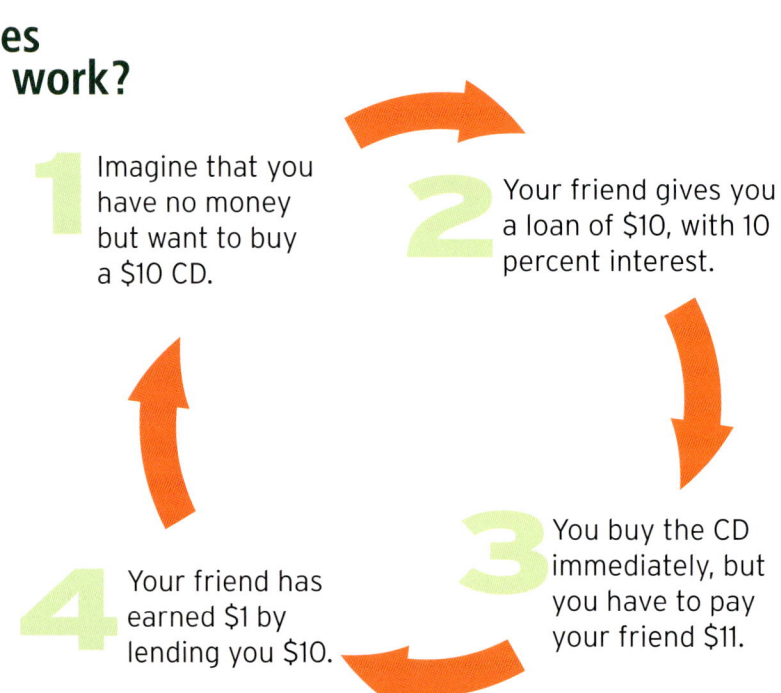

1. Imagine that you have no money but want to buy a $10 CD.
2. Your friend gives you a loan of $10, with 10 percent interest.
3. You buy the CD immediately, but you have to pay your friend $11.
4. Your friend has earned $1 by lending you $10.

What Happens When You Deposit a Check?

1 Deposit a check in the bank.

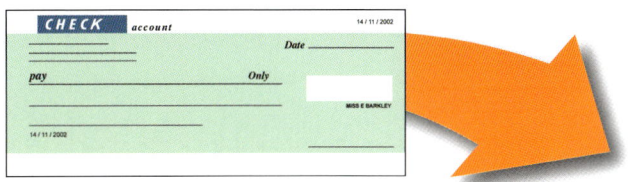

2 Your bank approves the check and sends it to the bank of the person who wrote the check.

3 The bank of the person who wrote the check deducts the amount written on the check from that person's account.

4 The money is deposited into your account. The transaction is complete.

BANKING VOCABULARY

ECONOMY the money and resources found in a certain place, such as a country

RECESSION a period of time when trade is reduced and the economy slows

Federal Reserve Bank

The Federal Reserve Bank sets the interest rates, or the amount of interest, that banks across the nation pay when they borrow money. The rate they set affects the entire **economy**.

When the interest rate is low, banks pay less to borrow money. They can pass these savings on to their customers. When interest rates are low, people are more likely to borrow money to buy cars, houses, and other items. This is good for the economy because it grows when people spend.

The Federal Reserve Bank is responsible for supervising banking policies and procedures across the nation. It also issues the national currency. There are twelve district Federal Reserve Bank locations across the United States, as well as a Board of Governors in Washington, DC.

The Board of Governors in Washington, DC, influence banking and money management policies for the entire nation.

Adjusting Interest Rates

Spending increases, and more people carry a debt. The pool of money for lending decreases.

The Federal Reserve increases the interest rate. This helps prevent unsafe borrowing and slows the economy.

Spending decreases. If the economy slows too much, there may be a recession.

The Federal Reserve decreases the interest rate. This makes it easier for people to borrow money and pay their debt.

23

BANKING VOCABULARY

OVERDRAFT a service that allows people to use more money than they have in their account

ATMs and Banking Cards

Today, people often use Automated Teller Machines, or ATMs, to do their banking. These machines offer most of the same services as human tellers inside banks. They allow customers to make deposits and withdrawals, as well as pay bills, at all hours of the day, any day of the week. ATMs can be found in many places, including malls, cruise ships, outside banks, at gas stations, and in hotels.

A debit card can be used to pay for goods and services in place of cash or checks. The cost of the purchase is automatically deducted from the purchaser's bank account. Therefore, people can only spend the money they have in their account unless they have an **overdraft** allowance. Many businesses, such as stores and restaurants, accept debit payments.

People can use plastic cards instead of cash to pay for products and services.

To use a debit card, a person needs a secret password, called a personal identification number (PIN). A PIN is a series of numbers that the account holder selects and must remember always.

The account holder is the only person who should know the PIN—not even the people working in the bank know this number. It is the only way to access money when using a debit card. It also keeps others from using another person's card. They cannot gain access to the funds if they do not know the secret password.

FAQ

How do people choose a PIN?
These are some tips for choosing a PIN that is secure and easy to remember.
- Some people find it difficult to remember PIN numbers. It may help to base your PIN on a word, such as your pet's name or your favorite color. Then, find the numbers on a telephone keypad that match the letters in your word.
- Often, you only need to use four numbers for your PIN. However, longer PIN numbers offer better protection from theft. For this reason, it is a good idea to use as many digits as your bank will allow.
- Try not to use the numbers of a birthday or another important date in the PIN. It is easy for someone who knows your birthday to guess your PIN.
- Once a PIN number has been chosen, do not write it down. If someone who has access to your debit card finds where you wrote down your PIN, he or she can use the number to access your money.

25

BANKING VOCABULARY

VIRTUAL only exists on the Internet or on a computer; does not have a physical form

Banking Technology

Today, technology plays a large role in banking. Most banks have a website where people can log in and do their banking online. Other banks are only available online. These **virtual** banks allow you to do all of your banking on the Internet. Since virtual banks do not have buildings and offices to maintain, they often have better rates. Virtual banks offer most of the same services as regular banks. People can open and close accounts, make investments, and borrow money.

SHOULD I BANK ONLINE?	
YES	**NO**
Virtual banks never close.	Internet connections must be secure.
Banking can be done any place there is Internet access.	Websites can be hard to use.
Transactions happen faster.	Takes time to set up account services.
Up-to-the-minute statements of accounts are available.	Limited human contact.

26

Banking Careers

There are many different jobs people do at banks. These are just a few examples.

Tellers

Tellers handle many of the basic transactions that take place inside a bank. They work directly with customers to take deposits, cash checks, pay bills and loans, and withdraw funds. At the start and end of their shift each day, tellers count the money they have on hand. Throughout the day, they must keep precise records of how this money is used. Tellers also provide customer service. They may answer basic questions about banking or arrange for customers to speak with someone who knows more about a certain type of bank product. To become a teller, you should have a high school diploma. Training often is provided at the bank. Tellers should enjoy working with people and have a good understanding of numbers.

Bank Managers

Bank managers supervise the day-to-day operations of the bank. They make sure that transactions are done properly based on the bank's standards. Bank managers hire new staff, train staff, and make work schedules. They ensure customers are pleased with the service they receive and deal with complaints. Bank managers set bank policies and create programs to attract new customers. To become a bank manager, you need a bachelor's degree in business administration from a university or college.

What Have You Learned?

1 What are banks?

2 Name three types of accounts.

3 How much money do banks keep on site?

4 What is interest?

5 What is the FDIC?

6 What is a checking account used for?

7 Which types of accounts earn the most interest?

8 Who can use a credit union?

9 When was the first U.S. central bank established?

10 How can you keep track of banking transactions?

Answers

1. Banks are financial institutions in which people can deposit their money for later use. People also can borrow money from banks.
2. Savings accounts, checking accounts, certificates of deposit
3. about three to 10 percent of the money they receive through deposits
4. money paid at a regular rate for the use of a loan
5. a U.S. government department that encourages people to use banks by insuring money stored there
6. to use money to make purchases and other transactions
7. certificates of deposit
8. only people belonging to these groups can put their money in a credit union
9. 1791
10. by reviewing bank statements or keeping a check register

29

What Does it Take to Start a Bank?

1. To start a bank, a person needs to write a business plan. This is a document that describes how the bank will work. It should include the roles of the key people working at the bank, the services the bank will provide, and long-term plans. A team of people who have a great deal of experience are needed to help build the bank.

2. Next, the person opening the bank needs to apply for a charter. A charter outlines the rules and regulations for the bank. A federal or state central banking system can issue a charter.

3. The next step to starting a bank is to decide where it will be located. An area that does not have any other banks nearby is best. If the bank is near others, it will need to offer special services that these banks do not have. This will help draw customers to the bank.

4. It takes a great deal of money to open a bank. A person needs to raise millions of dollars before the bank can open for business.

Starting a bank is a big responsibility. Imagine you are a successful businessperson and you want to open your own bank. Think about how you might raise the funds you need to open a bank. You may ask people to invest in your bank. What services will your bank offer?

Further Research

Many books and websites provide information on banking. To learn more about banking, borrow books from the library, or surf the Internet.

Most libraries have computers that connect to a database for researching information. If you input a key word, you will be provided with a list of books in the library that contain information on that topic. Nonfiction books are arranged numerically, using their call number. Fiction books are organized alphabetically by the author's last name.

Websites

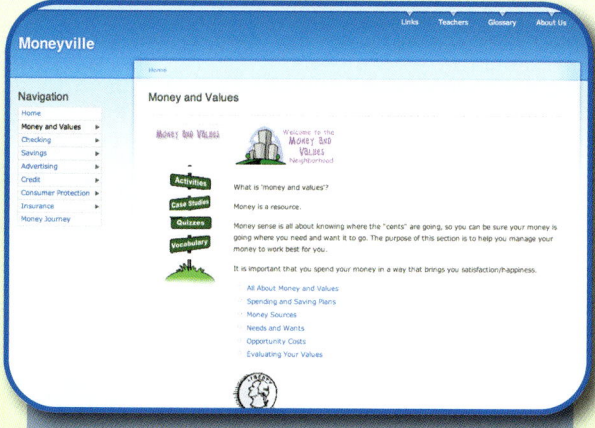

To find out more about how money works, visit

http://community.ca.uky.edu/ moneyville

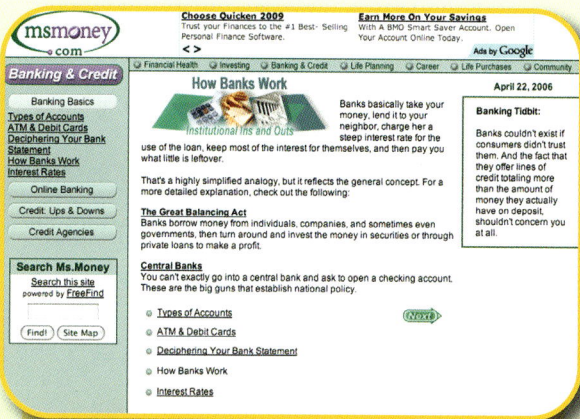

For more information about banking, check out

www.msmoney.com/mm/banking/ bkbasics/how_work.htm

Glossary

balance: the amount of money in an account

banknotes: paper money that acts as a promise to pay the sum upon request

barter: to exchange goods and services for other goods and services

bills: money owed for the use of goods or services

bonds: money a person lends to a company that earns more money over time

central bank: a bank that provides services for the nation's government

cleared: free of any reason why the money cannot be moved from one account to another

commercial: for the purpose of making a profit

commodities: items of value

credited: added to the sum of an account

currency: the type of money used in a certain country

debit card: a plastic card that is issued by a bank to a client that allows the client to access his or her account

debts: money owed

deducted: taken away or subtracted from an account

deposit: the act of putting money into a bank account; the sum of money in the account

economy: the money and resources found in a certain place, such as a country

endorsed: signed the back of a check to authorize the release of funds

exchange: to give something and receive another item

incentive: encouragement for someone to do something

insured: made arrangements to be repaid if money is damaged or stolen

interest: money paid at a regular rate for the use of a loan

investing: purchasing an item with the hope that it will be worth more someday

lend: to give something, such as money, with the understanding that it will be returned

overdraft: a service that allows people to use more money than they have in their account

principle: the value of money borrowed before interest

profit: money earned

recession: a period of time when trade is reduced and the economy slows

regulate: control or maintain

reserves: money on hold

statement: a document that shows all of the transactions, such as deposits and withdrawals, that have taken place over a period of time

stocks: pieces, or shares, of a company that can be bought, represented by a certificate

transactions: acts of business, such as buying or selling

transferred: moved funds from one person or business to another

virtual: only exists on the Internet or on a computer; does not have a physical form

withdrawn: taken out of any account

Index

account 4, 10, 11, 12, 13, 14, 15, 19, 21, 24, 25, 26, 28
ATM 5, 24

banknotes 8, 9
borrowing 4, 5, 16, 17, 20, 23 26, 29, 31

central bank 6, 7, 8, 11, 28, 30
certificates of deposit 12, 13, 29
checking 11, 12, 13, 14, 15, 28, 29

debit card 10, 13, 114, 19, 24, 25
deposit 4, 9, 10, 11, 12, 13, 14, 15, 18, 20, 21, 24, 27, 29

economy 22, 23

FDIC 13, 18, 28

interest 4, 5, 10, 11, 12, 13, 15, 16, 17, 19, 22, 23, 28
Internet 26, 31

savings 11, 12, 13, 17, 29
spending 12, 14, 22, 23, 24

transaction 12, 13, 15, 18, 19, 21, 26, 27, 28, 29